Shelly,
I pray that God will always bless you and your precious family.

Love,
Maryalayse
11/2016

A Mother's Prayers

for

Her High School Son

By~
MaryAlayne B. Long

Compiled By~
Jake Long

Copyright © 2013, 2015 MaryAlayne B. Long.

All rights reserved. No part of this book may be used or reproduced by any means, graphic, electronic, or mechanical, including photocopying, recording, taping or by any information storage retrieval system without the written permission of the publisher except in the case of brief quotations embodied in critical articles and reviews.

Author Credits: The Alabama Housewife

WestBow Press books may be ordered through booksellers or by contacting:

WestBow Press
A Division of Thomas Nelson & Zondervan
1663 Liberty Drive
Bloomington, IN 47403
www.westbowpress.com
1 (866) 928-1240

Because of the dynamic nature of the Internet, any web addresses or links contained in this book may have changed since publication and may no longer be valid. The views expressed in this work are solely those of the author and do not necessarily reflect the views of the publisher, and the publisher hereby disclaims any responsibility for them.

Any people depicted in stock imagery provided by Thinkstock are models, and such images are being used for illustrative purposes only.
Certain stock imagery © Thinkstock.

ISBN: 978-1-4908-3621-8 (sc)
ISBN: 978-1-4908-3620-1 (hc)
ISBN: 978-1-4908-3622-5 (e)

Library of Congress Control Number: 2014907895

Printed in the United States of America.

WestBow Press rev. date: 01/23/2015

This book is lovingly dedicated
to my wonderful children
Jake and SadieSue~
for making me realize the importance of prayer
in a way I never did before.

Foreword by~
Jake Long

This book was written by my Mom. If you have not had the pleasure of meeting my Mom then I can only feel sorry for you. I feel that way because you have missed out on meeting one of the kindest most generous and loving people you will ever meet. If you ever have the chance to meet her I strongly encourage you to do so. She will almost certainly greet you with a big smile and a welcoming, "How are you?". My Mom is the rare kind of person who cares more about the happiness of everyone around her rather than her own.

If you were to look at an official document about my family; my Mother would be listed as *unemployed*. I can assure you that is the largest understatement in the history of the world. My Mom is most certainly not unemployed. In fact she has what I would consider to be the most demanding and stressful job in the world, being my Mom. I promise you this is no easy task. I would not want to take care of "me"! Throw my sister's needs on top of mine and that makes for quite an impressive workload. *Unemployed* or not, she works harder than my Dad and he is the hardest workingman I know. I can see some of you reading this and thinking (Insert Snobby Voice) "Oh well.... I'm sure your mom works quite hard but I am a *doctor* and I am on call three times a week.". (To be clear, I have no ill will with doctors. I am just using this as an example.) On call three times a week? That is NOTHING! For 19 years my Mom has been on call **every hour of every day and night!** She is always ready to answer to my every waking whim. For 14 of those years she has been on call for not just one but TWO ungrateful children. For all our lives my mother has given every bit of love and care she has to my sister and me. She loves us both equally, and she loves us more than anything else on this earth. Her life is devoted to us and for that I am more thankful than I will ever be able to put into words.

I now feel it necessary to write a bit about myself. I do this only to advance the evidence of how well my Mom raised me. She taught me above all else to be humble so I assure you I am not bragging on myself by listing my accomplishments but rather on my Mother. I also want you to know that my Dad had an equally important role in raising me-- but he did not write this book so this is not about him. **(I Love You Dad!)** Throughout my life my Mom has always supported me in whatever I decided to pursue. Early in life that was a lot. Soccer, baseball, karate, basketball, guitar, you name it. I gave it all a try and my Mom was always right there encouraging me. Even though I tried it all, none of it was right for me. None of it was my *passion*. In 6th grade (at the request of my Dad and with my Mother's full encouragement) I reluctantly signed up for football. I was not what you would call "athletic" and was not sure I would be any good. I didn't even think I would like it. I was wrong. I found my passion. I may not have been the biggest or the best player on the field but I loved every minute I spent on it. From that moment on my life was dominated by football, and so was my Mom's. She gave the term "Team Mom" a whole new meaning. She made cakes and meals for the coaches, brought the team food, and my personal favorite-she made us special Bible cards each week. If you ask anyone on any team I have ever played football for they will know exactly who Jake's mom is. I am where I am today because of my Mother. If you ask her she will say it was all because of my hard work and determination but that is just the humble person she is. Nothing I have achieved in life would have been possible without her encouragement. I owe it all to my Mom.

The prayers you will be given the pleasure of reading in this book come in one of the simplest forms, a text message. Near the end of my sophomore year of high school I began to drive myself to school. I lived farther away than the majority of the other students attending my school and had to brave a 10 mile drive on the interstate. My loving nervous Mother demanded I text her upon my arrival. I thought it was stupid so upon arriving at Vestavia Hills High School for the first time under my own power, my sarcastic teenage self sent a simple one word text, "Here." What I received in return was not only a surprise to me but the start of a very long and still continued tradition between my Mother and me. I received my first morning prayer. Specifically,

> *"I pray that you know God has a plan for your life."*

From then on everyday I would drive to school and upon arrival text my short simple "Here". In return I would receive some sort of loving encouragement from my mom in the form of a prayer. These are the prayers I have compiled for you to read in this particular book. I hope that they provide you with as much encouragement and guidance as they have provided me.

In closing I would like to say that this book and it's wonderful life motivation were written entirely by my Mother. However, I would like to quickly add my one small speck of advice. If you ever feel lost in life and do not know what you are going to do with yourself I suggest but one thing to you. Listen to **"*If You Want To Sing Out Sing Out*" by Cat Stevens.** Just listen to that song and all shall fall into place. The point of the song is not to worry about the opinions or actions of others but rather just do what makes you happy. I hope you can gain some type of guidance from the prayers my Mother has blessed me with and I hope you too can find the path to being happy.

God Bless,
Jake Long

Matthew 23:12

Introduction by~
MaryAlayne B. Long

If you have just read the foreword to this book, then I'm not really sure you need me to add anything. First of all, after I finished reading it, I wasn't fully able to scrape myself up off the floor and focus my eyes well enough to write. To be clear--my son never has to buy another single gift for me....ever....for the rest of my life. Those words were all I need. Of course I know there are plenty of folks who work harder than I do. I can't begin to express the admiration I feel for single parents who work two and three jobs just to keep food on the table. However, knowing that my son feels that way about me is priceless. The fact that my husband and I have been able to raise a son who could write such things is possible because of only one thing-PRAYER. The peace we receive when we come to God in prayer is remarkable and not a day goes by that I don't pray for both of my children. I pray A LOT and I pray for all sorts of things. It's likely at some point I may have even prayed for you. I am a firm believer in prayer and this book is full of them. The prayers appear exactly as they were written and in the exact order they were sent. They directly relate to my relationship with my son and the things that were going on in our lives at the time they were written. They are words--not necessarily of wisdom--but of love and intended inspiration. A great many of them are repetitive, as prayers so often tend to be. Some of them are simple. Some of them are personal and may not make any sense to you whatsoever. However, know that they are based in love, faith and the knowledge that God understands them all. I am honored that Jake thought they were worthy of sharing and I am thankful that you are taking the time to read them.

I have always told my children that God puts them in the perfect places for their lives to stay on His path. It's their choice if they will use those platforms to serve Him or not. You and I have the same opportunity.

> I pray that we will all be brave enough to hear God's call
> and to answer with love and understanding.

With Love and Appreciation,
MaryAlayne

I pray because I can't help myself.
I pray because I'm helpless.
I pray because the need flows out of me all the time~
waking and sleeping.
It doesn't change God~it changes me.

C.S. Lewis

1. I pray that you know God has a plan for your life.

2. I pray that you will not be anxious about ANYTHING.

3. I pray God's word lives in your heart
and guides you on life's journey.

4. I pray that you are always aware of God's presence in your life, and that you know nothing can separate you from Him.

5. I pray that you look to God for wisdom.

6. I pray that you believe nothing is impossible with God.

7. I pray that you live your life with purpose.

8. I pray that we love one another as God has taught us to love.

9. I pray that you keep God's commandments and pass them down to your children.

10. I pray that you will be filled with a servants heart.

11. I pray that you can see God at work through your weakness and your struggles.

12. I pray that you let God's light shine through you.

13. I pray that you know God wants to give you more than you could ever dream or imagine!

14. I pray that you experience the peace of God.

15. I pray that God's spirit will shine through you.

16. I pray that you are aware
of God's love for you.

17. I pray that you will find time to
be still in the presence of God.

*18. I pray that you know God's goodness,
even when things don't seem so good.*

19. I pray that you count each day as a blessing.

20. I pray that you are able to trust God to provide all that you need each day.

21. I pray God's word lives in your heart and guides you on life's journey.

22. I pray that you let God's light shine through you.

23. I pray that you know God wants to give you more than you could ever dream or imagine.

24. I pray that you will always remember that although our world is always changing, GOD never changes.

25. I pray that you experience the peace of God.

26. I pray that God's spirit will shine through you.

27. I pray God's word lives in your heart and guides you on life's journey.

28. I pray that you count each day as a blessing!

29. I pray that you know what a blessing you have been to me for 17 years!!

30. I pray that you know how much you are loved!

31. I pray that you know how thankful I am for the wonderful memories we made this weekend!

32. I pray that you will be filled with a servant's heart.

33. I pray that you clearly see all the blessings
God places in your life each and every day.

34. I pray that you let God's light shine through you!

35. I pray that you always remember how blessed
you are and that you see all the ways
God shines His light on you each day!

36. I pray that you will be a blessing to others, as you are to me.

37. I pray that you know how much joy you bring to my life!

38. I pray that you know how blessed our family is—in so many ways.

39. I pray that you know how much joy you bring to my life each and every day!

40. I pray that you will not be anxious about anything.

41. I pray that you are thankful to God for the strong mind he gave you!

42. I pray that you take time to be still and know there is a God.

43. I pray that you feel better today. :)

44. I pray that you always
have a servants heart.

45. I pray that we love one another
as God has taught us to love.

46. I pray that you see God all around you,
each and every day.

47. I pray that you will never grow weary of doing what is right for The Lord.

48. I pray that you know ALL your blessings come through God.

49. I pray that you know how blessed I feel to be your mother.

50. I pray that you never let the place you start dictate the place you finish!

51. I pray that you will be the other fish.

52. I pray that you will encourage others to follow Jesus.

53. I pray that The Glory of The Lord will shine upon you!

54. I pray that you will be an ambassador for Jesus.

55. I pray that you will always follow God's path for your life.

56. I pray that you feel blessed today!

57. I pray that you follow God's path for your life.

58. I pray that you always know how much you are loved.

59. I pray that you know you are a great leader- and that you always lead in the proper direction.

*60. I pray that you know what a blessing it is to be as naturally SMART as you are.....
and that you never squander your gift.*

61. I pray that you stay on God's path for your life.

62. I pray that you love others as God has taught you.

63. I pray that you will experience the peace of God.

64. I pray that you know God's spirit shines through you.

65. I pray that you will keep your faith strong.

66. I pray that you love others as God loves you.

67. I pray that you know—a mother who cared nothing about you or your happiness would leave you with a very boring life.

68. I pray that you seek God's path for your life, everyday, for as long as you shall live.

69. I pray that God's grace will be with you now and always.

70. I pray that you count each day as a blessing.

71. I pray that you will always be humble.

72. I pray that you are always thankful for ALL the blessings in your life.

73. I pray that we love one another as God has taught us to love.

74. I pray that you will always be a leader for Jesus.

75. I pray that you know what a blessing it is to live in a free country.

76. I pray that you know God has a special plan for your life.

77. I pray that you know all things are possible with God!

78. I pray that you know how proud you make me-every single day.

79. I pray that you respect the holiness of this week-- when Christ prepared to give his life for you.

80. I pray that you live every day of your life as a humble, grateful, strong Christian man.

81. I pray that you know we are **ALL** sinners— saved by God's Amazing Grace!

82. I pray that you always seek to follow Christ--just as you do now.

83. I pray that the blessings of the risen Christ will surround you all of your life!

84. I pray that you take time to thank God for all the blessings in your life.

85. I pray that you keep God's commandments and pass them down to your children.

86. I pray that you have a grasp of just how much your parents love you.

87. I pray that you know God wants to give you more than you could dream or ever imagine.

88. I pray that you know God has chosen you

for something special!

89. I pray that you know-

if God brings you to it, He will guide you through it!

90. I pray that you always

have a passion for what you do.

91. I pray that you appreciate ALL the abilities

God has blessed you with!

92. I pray that you enjoy
each and every moment of your life!

93. I pray that you are grateful for
your strength of mind, body and spirit!

94. I pray that you keep a positive
attitude in all things.

95. I pray that you know what a blessing it is to be your mother!

96. I pray that you know how much I wish you would come to the beach!!!!

97. I pray that you seek to serve God first before all others.

98. I pray that you are grateful for all the challenges in your life- they build character.

99. I pray that you take time to be still….
and know there is a God!

100. I pray that you know how much
I love and appreciate you–
and how proud I am of you!

101. I pray that you know that God
has a great plan for your life!

102. I pray that you know

how grateful I am that

God chose me to be your mother!

103. I pray that the blessings in your life

are always visible to you.

104. I pray that you are

truly humble, grateful and thankful

for every breath you take.

105. I pray that you know what a wonderful life you lead.

106. I pray that you know God is always with you.

107. I pray that you seek first the kingdom of His love.

108. I pray that you praise God from whom all blessings flow!

109. I pray that you know how much
I love making breakfast for you!

110. I pray that you know how proud I am
of your Christian leadership.

111. I pray that you know God has given you the knowledge, skill and ability to ace your tests!

112. I pray that you keep God's commandments and pass them down to your children.

113. I pray that you know how
proud your parents are
of you and the choices you make.

114. I pray that you are always careful
and that you stay safe on this and
every day of your life.

115. I pray that you always remember—
to whom much is given, much is expected.

116. I pray that you rejoice in every
blessing God has given you!

117. I pray that you are thankful for the freedom to worship God freely.

118. I pray that you know- ANYTHING is possible with GOD!

119. I pray that you are always looking for God's plan- HE has a great one for your life.

120. I pray that you praise God
from whom all blessings flow.

121. I pray that you take time to be
still and know there is a God.

122. I pray that you know God wants to give you
more than you could ever dream or imagine.

123. I pray that you rejoice in The Lord!

124. I pray that you know

how much I trust you--

and how much I will miss you this week.

125. I pray that you

will be filled with a servants spirit.

126. I pray that you are always aware

of God's presence in your life

and that you know nothing can separate you from HIM!

127. I pray that you know how grateful I am

that God chose me to be your Mother!

128. I pray that you keep your faith
rooted in The Lord.

129. I pray that you know there is
a lesson from God
in each day of your life.

130. I pray that you know
hard work and dedication
are two traits I admire so much in you!

131. I pray that you will not be anxious about anything.

132. I pray that you know
how much joy you bring to my life.

133. I pray for you every blessing imaginable
on this and every day of your life!!

134. I pray that you are always grateful
for the gifts God has given you!

135. I pray that you are always humble
and helpful to everyone around you.

136. I pray that you know how
proud I am of you—
for so many different reasons!

137. I pray that God will guide you and keep you safe in all you do.

138. I pray that you know nothing is impossible with GOD!

139. I pray that you follow the path God has for your life!

140. I pray that you always remember
how blessed I feel to be your Mother.

141. I pray that you are always grateful
for the blessing of good health.

142. I pray that you know how special you are.

143. I pray that you know how much you are loved.

144. I pray that you will always remember that all things are possible through GOD!

145. I pray that you know how proud I am of your faith in God.

146. I pray that you will always seek to serve HIM first-before all else.

147. I pray that you use your gifts

to serve others.

148. I pray that you grateful to be an

AMERICAN

and to live in these United States!

**149. I pray that you know what a blessing it is to be loved by, cared for, attended to and trusted by your parents--who would (and often do) do anything for you.*

150. I pray that you know how blessed you are
that God chose your family for you.

151. I pray that you know
God has a wonderful plan for your life.

152. I pray that God will cover you
with healing power and grace!

153. I pray that you are an instrument for The Lord.

154. I pray that God will
continue to use you to help others.

155. I pray that you will be
God's steward and servant every day of your life.

156. I pray that you know
how blessed your Daddy and I are to be your parents!

157. I pray that you are always thankful for people who offer to do kind things for you.

158. I pray that you are always humble, grateful and thankful for all your many blessings.

159. I pray that you will always remember that God has a wonderful plan for your life!

160. I pray that you will always continue to lead by example.

161. I pray that you know
the shield of God is with you always!

162. I pray that you see
God's beauty in everything around you.

163. I pray that you enjoy the
wonderful fall weather!

164. I pray that you know
how much joy you bring to my life.

165. I pray that you seek to serve HIM first before all else.

166. I pray that you know how good it feels
when I know I have made you happy!!

167. I pray that you know how proud I am
of the young man you have become!

168. I pray that you know I am always here for you
no matter what you may need.

169. I pray that you see God in the simple things.

170. I pray that you pray-everyday.

171. I pray that you always find

the lesson in what God sends your way.

172. I pray that you stay safe on your journey.

173. I pray that you are always thankful for your sister.

174. I pray that you are never boastful but always humble, grateful and thankful for ALL your many blessings.

175. I pray that you know that
God has a great and mighty plan for your life!

176. I pray that you know
how proud you make me-in so many ways!

177. I pray that you know
what a blessing you are to me.

178. I pray that you appreciate your Mother.

179. I pray that you experience the Peace of God.

180. I pray that you are always grateful
for the gifts that God has given you!

181. I pray that you are thankful for your good health
and that you never take it for granted.

182. I pray that you know how
much joy you bring to my life!

183. I pray that you always know that
God has a special plan for your life.

184. I pray that you always
trust God for all you need each day.

185. I pray that you always
think before you speak,
look before you leap and pray before you eat or sleep.

186. I pray what that you know what a blessing it is to have married parents who love each other, love you, and want to support you in your activities and be involved in your life.

187. I pray that you know how blessed you are to have two parents that always want the best for you.

188. I pray that you know
what a blessing it is to be an American.

189. I pray that you
are always a strong leader for The Lord.

190. I pray that you know God is always on your side.

191. I pray that you are grateful for your parents who

revolve around you and who--

by the way---

we're married 19 years ago today.

192. I pray that you know

what a blessing it is for me to be your Mother.

193. I pray that you know you are a child of God—

and that is the greatest thing anyone can be.

194. I pray that you know how incredibly proud I am of you

for so many reasons I simply don't have enough words.

I love you more than you will ever know!!

195. I pray that you are able to understand how proud we are of you for EARNING your place today. You are one of our greatest blessings.

196. I pray that you know how amazed I am by you.

197. I pray that you know God's plan for your life is mighty and great!

198. I pray that you know I am praying for you.

199. I pray that you know this is just the beginning.

200. I pray that you love rainy days as much as I do. They bring growth and teach us to appreciate the sun.

201. I pray that you are preparing to enjoy the CHRISTmas season.

202. I pray that you know you can do anything you put your mind to.

203. I pray that you know what a blessing it is to have a warm and loving home.

204. I pray you are thankful for the blessing of good health.

205. I pray that you always seek to serve those who are less fortunate than you.

206. I pray that you know how thankful I am to have such a trustworthy son.

207. I pray that you know it's okay
to take it easy when you are sick.

208. I pray that you know
how blessed I am to be your mother.

209. I pray that you know how blessed our family is.

210. I pray that you know how proud I am of your faithfulness to God.

211. I pray that you know how much your sister loves you.

212. I pray that you know

what a blessed life we all have.

213. I pray that you know

how much I love you.

214. I pray that you are grateful for your good mental health.

215. I pray that you recognize what a charmed life you lead.

216. I pray that your new year will be blessed
in more ways than you can imagine!!

*217. I pray that you know God gives you
a lesson in every situation.
It's up to you whether you learn it or not.*

218. I pray that you know

how much I appreciate the person you are.

219. I pray that you know

how proud I am of the Gentleman you have become.

220. I pray that you know

how much I appreciate your reasonable-ness.

221. I pray that you know regardless if your circumstances,

God gives YOU the choice to make good decisions.

222. I pray that you know how grateful I am

God chose me to be your Mother!

223. I pray that you know, even when I am crazy busy,

you are ALWAYS in my thoughts!!

224. I pray that you know what a blessing it is
to be in good health.

225. I pray that you know
I will always be an over protective mother.
But the "good kind" of over protective.

226. I pray that you know there are worse things
you could do than to take advice from your Mother.

227. I pray that you know how much you are loved.

228. I pray that you know how happy it
makes me to make you happy.

229. I pray that you know what a privileged life you live
and that you are grateful for it.

230. I pray that you know how proud
I am of your good judgement
and how much I trust you.

231. I pray that you know
there's nothing that can replace
a group of really good friends.
You are blessed indeed!!

232. I pray that you know how much I love you.

233. I pray that you know,
good things come to those who wait.

234. I pray that you are always true to yourself.

235. I pray that you know how proud you make me, each and every day!!

236. I pray that you always drive safely.

237. I pray that you always keep your eyes on the path that God has for your life.

238. I pray that you are blessed
by your knowledge of God's love for us all.

239. I pray that you know what a blessing you are to my life.

240. I pray that you know what a blessing it is
to have a responsible, trustworthy son!

241. I pray that you know I so appreciate every part of you and the place you hold on our family.

242. I pray that you know I am always praying for you.

243. I pray that you know that ANY young lady would be lucky indeed to go with you to the prom.....
Or anywhere else for that matter!

244. I pray that you are always humble,

grateful and thankful

for all your many blessings.

245. I pray that you know

what a great plan God has for your life!!

246. I pray that you know how much I admire your discipline.

247. I pray that you never loose sight
of the plan God has for you!

248. I pray that you know;
"He that dwelleth
in the secret place of the most High
shall abide under the shadow of the Almighty."
Psalm 91:1

249. I pray that you will prosper despite every difficulty
that may come your way. Don't just survive, THRIVE!

250. I pray that you will remember that although our world is always changing, God never changes.

251. I pray that you are able to trust God to provide all that you need each day!

252. I pray that you know God wouldn't give you a dream unless He already had a plan to make it a reality.

253. I pray that you know
God's goodness and mercy
will follow you all the days of your life!

254. I pray that you know you are one of
the most important things in my life and that
I will NEVER STOP
worrying about you and protecting you.

255. I pray that you know I will always try
not only to help you become a better man
but also help myself become a better mother.
I love you more than you could ever know.

256. I pray that you are careful and wise.

257. I pray that you know
when you focus on being a blessing to others,
God makes sure you are always abundantly blessed.

258. I pray that you know choosing to be positive and having a grateful attitude is going to determine how you're going to live your life.

259. I pray that you seek to honor God in all that you do.

260. I pray that you know how much you are loved.

261. I pray that you are always grateful for the opportunities God gives you to set an example for Him.

262. I pray that you know choosing to be positive and having a grateful attitude is going to determine how you are going to live your life.

263. I pray that you know I never cease to give thanks for you and always remember you in my prayers.

264. I pray that you never question God but that you always TRUST him.

265. I pray that you never forget the debt Jesus paid for ALL of us on this most HOLY day.

266. I pray that you know how much joy you bring to my life.

267. I pray that you are always as eager to serve The Lord as you are now.

268. I pray that you may not only love, but that you always feel loved.

269. I pray that you always strive to give more than you take.

270. I pray that you know God always has the best plan.

271. I pray you know how much I appreciate YOU!!

272. I pray that you know how blessed you are.

273. I pray that you maintain your positive attitude!

274. I pray that you know the harvest is greatest
for those who work hardest.

275. I pray that you always try
to give more and take less.

276. I pray that you know how much I love you.

277. I pray that you know God
is in charge of everything.

278. I pray that you always
remember who you are.

279. I pray that you always know
worry is not necessary when God is in charge.

280. I pray that you seek ye first
the kingdom of His love
and make Him first in everything you do.

*281. I pray that you always stand up for what's right...
Even when what's right isn't what's easy.*

282. I pray that you know
how much joy you bring to my life!

283. I pray that you know what
a blessing you are to me.

284. I pray that you are always
grateful for your health.

285. I pray that you are always grateful
for the gifts God gives you.

286. I pray that you are always humble.

287. I pray that you are always grateful for the path that has been cut for you and proud of the legacy that is yours.

288. I pray that you are always kind.

289. I pray that you are always faithful to God before all else.

290. I pray that you never doubt your own self worth.

291. I pray that you always focus on the joy in your life.

292. I pray that you always try to be kind.

293. I pray that you know

I always have your best interest at heart.

294. I pray that you are always strong in your faith.

295. I pray that you know this is only just the beginning.

Acknowledgements

I have always loved to write. I think it's part of being Southern. There's something about the smell of honeysuckle, the taste of sweet tea, the feel of bare feet in freshly plowed dirt and the way a baby looks in a hand smocked day gown that has been handed down for three generations that lulls your senses into submission and makes you want to put your thoughts on paper. For those reasons (and for others too numerous to name) several years ago, I started writing a book. It's a collection of short essays really--that I have wanted to publish for quite some time. The first chapter in that as yet unpublished book is called "Surely The Presence". It comes from the title of my most favorite hymn and it speaks to my view that if you put God first in your life, everything else will fall into place. I suppose it is only fitting that this collection of prayers found its way to the printing press before my other book did. Putting God first has never failed me and it is only when I sit him on the back burner of my life that my pot starts to boil over. I am thankful to The Lord in more ways than I can say. If any part of this book can be used to honor Him, I will be forever grateful.

I'll be honest with you-when I started sending these prayers to my son, I didn't even know for sure that he was reading them. Not for a very long time. Then one day when I was traveling, I received a text from him reminding me that he hadn't received a prayer that day. It read simply "Prayer?". Of course, I sent one immediately. It made me so happy to know that he not only was reading the prayers each day but that he was also *waiting* for them. Learning that you have successfully lead your child to wait for The Lord is a wonderful gift that I can hardly describe.

When Jake moved to college--4 days after high school graduation--it was an exciting day. He and I went together with his truck and my SUV both fully loaded. For folks that know me it will come as NO surprise that the first thing I did upon my arrival at his dorm was to hang drapes and re-arrange the furniture. My husband says he has never encountered anyone who gets as much enjoyment out of moving furniture as I do! I also love to "fluff" a room, so I made the bed, helped put away clothes, set up the TV and put towels in the bathroom---monogrammed, of course. I stayed busy doing the things I love to do and before I knew it, the day was gone. We had such a fun time and I actually managed to laugh my way through the day instead of cry....until I got in the car to drive home. I made it almost all the way to Bryant Drive before the tears started to roll. To be clear; that means I drove about 50 feet. I listened to a few of our favorite songs, a few of my favorite songs, a few obligatory tear-jerkers and then I cut myself off. As one friend had said to me earlier that week--"If you have raised up your child in the way they should go, and then you are sad when they go that way; it's mighty selfish.". Whew--tough but true words--and ones I needed to hear. I made it back in one piece and woke up the next day still very much alive. Amazingly, even though I had tortured myself by listening to **He Stopped Loving Her Today**....the ultimate tear-jerking song....I had not driven into a ditch on the way home. I woke up, made coffee and sat in a quiet house that was minus one child. One child that--if all things go as they should--would never be a permanent resident of my home again. So what is a Mother to do? Pray. I sent him his first "college prayer" that day. It was a reflex almost--getting up and sending that prayer to him each school day. I don't know that I could do without it at this point. It is as much for me as it is for him.

Several weeks later, I received a call from Jake. If you are anything like me--when a child calls home from college the world stops. You start telling everyone to be quiet; turn off the TV or the radio; get up and leave the table or the room; leave the checkout line at the Piggly Wiggly; run out of the beauty parlor with tinfoil in your hair...... When they make time for you at this stage in their lives you are elated. HALT--my child is calling! So in my quiet moment of excitement--I was greeted with these words. "Hey--did you know you wrote a book?". Well yes, I believe I did know that. It's still on my computer (and partially in my head) but yes, I know. Jake has wanted me to publish that book for quite some time so I honestly thought he was calling to harass me about my procrastination. "No--not that book." he said. "A prayer book.". Well no, I don't believe I know anything about that! It just so happens that he was not only reading the prayers I sent each day-he was saving them. He took the time, on his own, between 6 a.m. workouts and daily classes and afternoon practices to type them up neatly and call a publisher. He had already made all of the arrangements to have this book published before I had any idea about it. I was shocked. It is rare that I am rendered speechless and that was indeed a rare moment. I honestly didn't know what to say. I can now tell you that working with Jake to get this book published has been a wonderful and enjoyable adventure I never dreamt I would take. It is a time that I will always treasure.

I can't end without thanking my dear sweet friend Missy Ballantyne. Although I don't get to see Missy nearly as often as I would like; I can easily say she is one of the sweetest, most kind and loving ladies I have ever had the pleasure to meet. She is a loving wife, mother and grandmother (YiaYia, actually--though you would never believe it to look at her--she is ageless and GORGEOUS!). She is a loyal and faithful friend and one of the most amazing hostesses I have ever had the pleasure to meet! She is also a wonderfully gifted photographer and a faithful follower of The Lord. One Christmas, Missy's sweet friend Dr. Kay Crosby gave her a jar filled with prayers. Missy later paired Kay's words of love and encouragement with her own amazing photographs to create the precious, beautiful book _Prayers for You: Prayers to Encourage and Inspire_. That book was my jumping off point for sending these prayers to Jake. It was after reading it that I actually felt led to send him a prayer each day. In fact, many of Kay's original prayers from Missy's book appear in this one. I have turned to it many times; indeed for encouragement and inspiration. If you don't have it in your library, you need to add it. Trust me! You can find her work at missyballantynephotography.com. The fact of the matter is, while I was inspired and encouraged by Missy, she was inspired and encouraged by yet another friend. Prayer does that you know. It encourages and inspires. It heals and it helps. It can be loud or it can be quiet. It can be public or it can be private. Prayer knows no boundaries and it sees no impossible situation.

It is my hope that this book might inspire you to pray for someone. Maybe you'll pray for someone you've never prayed for before--or for someone you don't really even want to pray for. Or maybe it will cause you to pray for someone you love in a new and different way. Maybe it will cause you to pray for yourself--for God to use you, change you, heal you. Whatever you get out of this book, I pray that it will lead you to see the Lord and the magnificent ways He can change your life if you'll only let Him.

Many Blessings~
MaryAlayne